CONTI

Published by History & Social Action Publications 2004
for Oxford House, Bethnal Green
& the Settlements & Social Action Research Group

History & Social Action Publications
20 Newburn St
London, SE11 5PJ
www.seancreighton.co.uk

ISBN No. 0-9548943-0-8

Oxford House
Derbyshire Street
London, E2 6HG

Tel: 020 7739 9001
email: info@oxfordhouse.org.uk
www.oxfordhouse.org.uk

Settlements & Social Action Research Group
www.seancreighton.co.uk

Picture credits
Front cover: Peter Kuenstler 1948. © Peter Kuenstler
Back cover: © Peter Kuenstler
Pages 21.24   © Oxford House

Printed and bound in Great Britain by
Uniprint Limited, 36 Jaggard Way, London SW12 8SG.

Foreword

It is a pleasure for me as the present Warden of Keble College, Oxford, to contribute this short foreword to the fascinating memoir about Oxford House written by Peter Kuenstler. One suspects that the founders of Oxford House, who set out full of hopes and ideals from Keble in 1884, would have been surprised or even taken aback that a woman should have been elected exactly one hundred years later as the eleventh Warden. Nor indeed as Mandy Ashworth wrote in the centenary year of Oxford House, would James Adderley, one of the first Heads, have been able to imagine a woman head of Oxford House.

Nevertheless I like to think that the founders would approve this renewal of the connection between Keble and Oxford House. Certainly after reading Peter's memoir I feel that they would recognise the spirit of the important, even if different, work that still goes on under the auspices of Oxford House to the benefit of the local community in Bethnal Green.

Oxford House was the first settlement to open its doors. In a way it had been founded in a hurry, to meet the fear felt by some at the time that the proposed University Settlement, which was to become Toynbee Hall, would lack a sufficiently High Anglican dimension. The names still visible on the brass plates in the chapel read like a roll call of the great and the good of the day, many of them familiar to me from the early history of my own College. A large portrait of A.F. Winnington-Ingram hangs in our common room to this day. The zeal of these men and many who followed them to help the working class, while also setting an example of a 'simple and religious life', nowadays seems very antiquated in its conception. Yet it went along with a real and successful determination to do something about the horrendous conditions they found in Bethnal Green in the 1880s.

Times change, and needs with them, and it is amazing to think that Oxford House is still thriving on the same site today, 120 years after it first opened. Youth work and social outreach are as important as ever and new communities have moved into the area. The new performance space and facilities are making all kinds of new and exciting things possible. But as Peter Kuenstler vividly shows in these reminiscences, a long history and many personal stories lie in the period between 1884 and 2004. They make inspiring reading.

In particular, Peter gives a fascinating and colourful account of life at Oxford House during World War II, when he came to work there with Guy Clutton-Brock. Guy was another inspirational figure who went on after the war to a very distinguished career opposing white supremacy in Southern Rhodesia. His vision for the House included activities not just for men and boys but for all ages and both sexes, with a governing system with wide community participation. The House also played an active part in a wide range of initiatives and organisations formed in those years before the welfare state. Peter Kuenstler's own work at Oxford House from 1940 to 1948 led to a long and fruitful career in youth work and community development and as a UN adviser in many countries. In these ways what went on at Oxford House influenced the wider world.

Oxford House has always had the ability to reinvent itself as the needs of Bethnal Green have changed. Led in recent years by Kim Adams, it has become a vibrant local centre, tuned in to the wider settlement movement of the 21st century, and the home of *oh!art*. The physical conditions in the House are very different from those of the 1940s, but the spirit is the same. There is every possible reason to think that the next 120 years will be just as enterprising and successful as the first.

Averil Cameron
Warden, Keble College, Oxford
Oxford House Development Trust

Chapter 1
Historical and
Geographical Preamble

The Oxford House in Bethnal Green was opened in the disused St Andrew's school in October 1884; there were two residents and room for two more; activities were a boys club, a library, Sunday afternoon lectures and Sunday evenings 'for a chat and smoke'. One large room upstairs was divided into cubicles and the club room was downstairs. At almost the same time Toynbee Hall started work in the Whitchapel distict of the neighbouring Borough of Stepney. This was the beginning of the settlement movement.

Settlements, places where groups of educated young men would live among the poor slum dwellers of the big cities, were the idea of the Rev. Samuel Barnett. He had been vicar of Whitechapel for some years and felt that the established church was out of touch and failing those in need both economically and culturally. During the early 1880s he made a number of visits to the Oxford and Cambridge colleges in which he appealed to the men there to 'come and be the squires of East London' after their graduation. They could work in the City or the civil service by day and in their spare time spread culture and light where it was most needed. There was an enthusiastic response in Oxford and, with the support of men like Cosmo Lang of Balliol College (later to become Archbishop of Canterbury), Toynbee Hall came into being in Whitechapel.

Believing that the new settlement should be outside the church Barnett resigned from his clerical post to become the first Warden of Toynbee Hall. There was, however, also a group of senior Oxford men, led by the Warden of Keble College, who felt it imperative that any such endeavour should be within the Anglican Church and their concern led to the creation of Oxford House in Bethnal Green. Not unnaturally Barnett was deeply pained by the split.

By 1891, the work of the House had grown to such an extent that a new custom – built building was urgently required both to house the increasing number of residents and for the Oxford House mens club. Following a public appeal the present building was completed and opened in 1892. By this time the Webbe Boys Club had been functioning in its own building in an old warehouse in Hare (Cheshire) Street. The Club was named after H. H. Webbe, a well-known cricketer. The University Mens and Boys Clubs were active in Victoria Park Square. Soon after the Repton Boys Club was started 'for a lower type of boy than the Webbe Institute'. There were numerous other developments started and run by the residents; a mutual loan club, a labour registry, a provident society, a house of shelter, bible classes, university extension lectures, the poor man's lawyer and many others. The list reads like a nursery of the social seedlings which were to grow into the flourishing plants of the 20th century welfare state.

The 1890s were a period of expansion of the activities and influence of the Oxford House under the Rev. Winnington Ingram. Side by side with the local activities, the House became a vital place for would-be ordinands in the Church of England to come for training and to test their calling. In the early years there had been a rapid turnover of Heads, but Winnington Ingram provided stability and continuity until he left in 1897 to become Bishop of Stepney, and later Bishop of London. His predecessor as Head had been the Rev. Hensley Henson, who later became a somewhat controversial Bishop of Durham. He had been the first and very successful Manager of the Webbe Boys Club from its foundation in 1888.

Another Anglican 'high flyer' who became Head for a short period after being a very popular boy's club leader was 'Dick' Sheppard, who became a well-known vicar of St Martin in the Fields, For some time William Temple (later Archbishop of Canterbury) was Secretary of the Oxford Committee which supported the work in Bethnal Green. It seems that alongside the many activities in Bethnal Green, the House helped to provide effective leaders for the Anglican Church.

Another significant development was the opening in 1891 of a 'sister' settlement for ladies in Victoria Park Square. St. Margaret's House had support both from Oxford and from Cheltenham Ladies' College. St. Margaret's soon became independent, with a girls club and other activities on its premises.

The early part of the 20th century brought more difficult times for the Oxford House. First the Boer War, and then more drastically the 1914-18 War, made it more and more difficult to attract residents and also to find an ordained Head of the House. As a result in 1916 Douglas Eyre, a long time resident became the first lay Head. He was succeeded by a clergyman, but he, like several of his predecessors stayed only a few years. There was a continuing unresolved ecclesiastical problem of how the work of the House should fit into the religious and social activities of the local parishes.

It appears that this difficulty continued as time went on even with the appointment of another long time resident layman Michael Seymour as Head. He remained until his death in 1937 during a period of much social tension and unrest, including the General Strike in 1926. In the previous year Seymour had been elected to the Bethnal Green Borough Council as an Independent member. Although the Council was Labour controlled he was elected Mayor in 1925 as a result of a split between factions within Labour, but he lost his seat in the 1934. During Seymour's time, the Rev. Kenneth Carey, a Webbe Club manager, was appointed as House Chaplain. Later he became Head of Westcott House.

Soon after the outbreak of WW2 in 1939, the Oxford House was virtually shut down. The Head, Rev. John Lewis, who had been appointed in 1937, had married in 1938. This event led to the resignation of Lord Hugh Cecil from the Council, since he felt that the House should remain a male celibate institution. Lewis had already broken the male-only tradition soon after his arrival by installing a resident matron and a resident cook to meet the needs of the 15 or so residents. Some of them were training as ordinands. Others had jobs in the City, and acted as volunteer club managers in the evenings, thus retaining the original idea of 'settlers' as proposed by Canon Barnett.

Chapter 2
Oxford House in 1940

In 1940 when mothers and children from Bethnal Green were evacuated to the country, Lewis and his wife decided to go with them.

As a 'caretaking' measure the Council agreed to appoint Guy Clutton-Brock as Head. He accepted the job while retaining his post as the head of the newly established Probation Service in the Home Office. He moved into the House with his wife Molly. There were a few other residents including: Neville and Nancy Scorah. Neville had a daytime job as an accountant and ran the Repton Boys Club in premises some distance to the east of the House. Katherine (K) White was the bursar and ran the financial side of things. She had joined the staff some years earlier as secretary to Michael Seymour. She remained for many years as the person who provided continuity and stability throughout the war and post war years. She was a devout Christian and regularly attended service at the Red Church in Bethnal Green Road, for which Rev. Douglas Lott was responsible. Lott was a frequent visitor to the House. Early in 1940 Hugh Kenyon, who had previously been one of the Managers (as Youth Workers were then called) at the Webbe Boys Club, was temporarily released from the Borstal Service in which he worked to return to run the club again in its original building. However, both Scorah and Kenyon left within a year or two, the former to join the RAF and the latter to return to the Borstal Service (and in post-war years to have a distinguished career in the Prison Service).

Other permanent residents were Reginald Johnson, John Raven and John Peterson all of them Conscientious Objectors. Reginald came from one of the best known families in the Potteries, the name of whose firm Johnson and Johnson can be found on millions of cups, plates and saucers. He had failed to convince the C.O. tribunal of the genuineness of his objection and been imprisoned for some months before being released on health grounds. His health continued to be problematic during his time at the House before he eventually left to take his place in the family firm. John Raven had a brilliant career as a classical scholar at Trinity College, Cambridge, and had been exempted from military service by a C.O. tribunal. In post-war years he returned to Cambridge and became Fellow and Dean of King's College and an authority on the works of Plato and the pre-Socratic philosophers, as well as a leading field botanist.

His father Canon Charles Raven, who was Master of Christ's College, Cambridge and a well-known Christian pacifist, had met Guy Clutton-Brock through the Christian Frontier, a club formed by J.H. Oldham who was a leading ecumenical figure. Through this contact John Raven had joined Oxford House and was given the task of helping in the running of the boys club which was attached to the mens club run in the premises in Victoria Park Square. These clubs' premises were next to a 17th century house which was then known as University House and was part of Oxford House. For a short while John Peterson, who had studied psychology at London University, was a resident in Oxford House. Then he went to live in University House and over the years developed it into an independent settlement with close links with and financing by Bethnal Green Borough Council. At the outbreak of war the premises of the Repton Boys Club had been taken over by the army. The Club moved into the University Club premises under the leadership of George Desert a former member.

When I started as a cleaner in 1940 the physical aspect of the House was much the same as it had been when it was built some 90 years earlier. There was a large entrance hall with a couple of small offices on the right as you entered. In one of these the hall porter, Mr. Braeger, was to be found when he was not testily trying to stop small children from playing on the front steps. On the left a short passage way alongside the staircase led to a large cloakroom with WCs and washbasins. At the end of the main entrance hall there was the common room furnished rather like a West End Club. To the left was the library and to the right the dining room. At the far end of the dining room was a staircase leading down to the basement. Half way down it was a door that opened into the small Hall. The basement, which throughout the war years became a key part of the House, contained the kitchen and two other rooms as well as a coal cellar, a large central heating boiler and a W.C. Both from the kitchen and from the front of the main stairs there were doors which opened out into a small backyard. From this yard were some steps for the tradesman's back entrance from Mape Street.

On the first and second floors were a series of interlocking L-shaped bed-sitting rooms and a communal bathroom for each floor. On the first floor the room facing the top of the stairs had been converted into the Head's study and office. The room at the far end of the passage was the main office with a small telephone switchboard, filing cabinets and a high old-fashioned desk at which K White did the books, standing up or perched on a high stool. On the third (top) floor there were two bed-sitting rooms, the chapel and two self-contained flats for the Head and Vice-Head of the House. The design of the House was intended to resemble that of a small Oxford College in which each resident would have his bed-sitting room, but all would share the rather limited washing facilities and would meet in the common room, the dining room and the library, while, below the stairs the non-resident domestic staff would have a sitting room, next to the kitchen.

The Oxford House mens club had separate, adjoining premises which were approached through a door in Derbyshire Street. Inside a door on the left, which led to the small hall, had in the past been kept locked except when one of the club managers wished to get into the club or return back into the House. A pair of swing doors on the right from the street entrance led into the larger Holland Hall, at the far end of which there was a stage. Behind it was a small, dark and smelly warren of changing rooms and showers. Facing the street entrance a steep flight of stairs led up to the main clubroom and canteen with a bar and small kitchen, and a WC. The bar served tea, cakes and cigarettes which were sold by a club member. The tea was made and the washing up done by Jack Hayes, who had been a cleaner at the Webbe. An ex-serviceman who had lost a leg in the First World War Hayes looked and acted like a Punch cartoon of a Cockney, cloth cap and all. Next to the canteen was a so called library. It had some shelves with a few rarely touched books and was usually used for playing cards. Alcohol and gambling were formally forbidden on club premises. From the canteen stairs led up to the billiard room with three full-sized billiard tables and a table tennis table. From there more stairs up to two small rooms at the top which were rarely used for discussions or rehearsals etc. The club building was designed as separate from the residence, the only connection being through the small hall.

Above the whole building and reached from the third floor of the House was the flat roof from which there was an extensive view. To the south were the arches carrying the main LNER railway line out of Liverpool Street with a large junction at the foot of Mape Street. These arches constituted a kind of frontier with Whitechapel and Stepney, even though in fact a few of the streets further south were still part of the borough of Bethnal Green. To the east the nearby Peabody Trust tenements stood up over the streets of small houses, beyond them the factory buildings of the chief local employer, the pharmaceutical firm of Allen and Hanbury. To the north east there were factory chimneys, one of which belonged to a soap or perfume maker from which on some days we would be assailed by sickly sweet smells. More often the smells were bitter and sour because we had as more immediate neighbours a pickle factory. The northern border of the view and effectively of the neighbourhood to which we were confined for most of the war years was the Hackney Road.

Chapter 3
The Blitz in Bethnal Green

In 1940 the Council of the House still had strong personal links to both the Anglican Church and Oxford. Financial links to the University were almost non-existent save for the Below Bridges Club. The Chairman of the Council was Sir Walter Moberly, Chairman of the University Grants Committee, the body which allocated Government grants to universities. He was a former Rector of Lincoln College, Oxford. Churchmen included his brother Robert Moberly, who was Bishop of Stepney, Canon George Cockin, who was Vicar of St Mary's, the University Church at Oxford, the Rev. Jack Markham, a former resident, and Prebendary Sarel, who was at St John's Church in Bethnal Green. Other former residents or club managers were Sir Vincent Baddeley, retired Secretary to the Board of Admiralty, Sir Henry Markham who had succeeded Sir Vincent to that post, and Sir Wyndham Deedes. Of these only two lived in Bethnal Green, Prebendary Sarel and Deedes. The latter visited the House frequently during the Blitz years in his capacity of Chief Air Raid Warden for the Borough.

Wyndham Deedes was a remarkable person. He had had a distinguished career first in the British Army, and then as chief of the Turkish Gendarmerie, which extended over all the Ottoman Empire. He became fluent in Turkish, which proved valuable during the 1914-18 war when again he served in the British Army. Later in Palestine under General Allenby he held a high administrative post until he retired at the age of 40 in 1923.

He came to live in Bethnal Green first as a resident in the House and then as Vice-Head. Later he moved to live with his mother in one of the large old houses in Victoria Park Square. He became active in social work, especially in the London and National Councils of Social Service, which came into existence during the 1920s. Much impressed by the example of the 'village houses' introduced in Turkey by Kemal Ataturk, he strongly supported the development of community centres in England. He was also secretary of the Association of Residential Settlements.

The House Council did not meet very often during the war years, because after his appointment as Head it entrusted things to Guy Clutton-Brock, who met from time to time with Walter Moberly and Wyndham Deedes. They accepted his decision to take young pacifists as resident workers.

The Below Bridges Club was an undergraduate club started in the early thirties at Oxford. The name was taken from the title of a then recently published book by one of the club managers from the Oxford and Bermondsey Boys Clubs. Its purpose was to raise interest among undergraduates and to raise funds which would be distributed among the different Settlements which had connections with Oxford. In 1940 Guy Clutton-Brock came to talk to the Club. Then in my second year at Oxford I attended one of these talks. I had in fact met Guy on several occasions before then. He had come to Rugby School in the late thirties to speak about his work as the head of the newly created Probation Service, which had been formed to take over from the old police court missionaries. We were required to attend this meeting, just as we were expected to make an annual donation to the work of the Rugby Clubs in Notting Hill. Guy was not a good speaker to school boys. I came to know him better when in the two following years we were both volunteer helpers at the Rugby Clubs Summer Camp at Rhymney on the Kent coast.

At the Below Bridges Club meeting in Oxford, Guy issued invitations to come to Oxford House for a weekend conference which was to be held to coincide with the end of the Hilary (summer) term at the University. Four or five of us decided to go. It was my introduction to the Oxford House and it was an exhilarating experience. The speakers included Canon Charles Raven, Canon George Cockin, Sir Wyndham Deedes and Derek Prince, a Cambridge graduate who had started an inter-racial school in Palestine for young Arabs and Jews. The theme of the weekend was a publication of the Christian Frontier club, entitled 'Europe in Travail'. The discussion focused on what kind of society was needed after the war. It took place at the time the German Army was invading Holland, Belgium and France. The evacuation of the British Army from Dunkirk was also taking place. The excitement of the high-level intellectual input was effectively moderated by the presence of a number of local mens club members who helped to turn the discussions to the realities of life in the East End.

Some months earlier I had been exempted from military service by a Conscientious Objectors tribunal on condition that I continued my studies (Ancient Latin and Greek and Philosophy) and did two nights a week fire watching. This involved keeping awake and armed with a bucket of sand and a bucket of water, on the alert in case incendiary bombs were dropped. I have never understood the logic of this decision. After the weekend in Bethnal Green I returned to my home in Hendon where I tried, in vain, to apply myself to vacation reading of Plato and Aristotle. After two weeks I gave it up and went down to Bethnal Green and pleaded with Guy Clutton-Brock to let me stay at the House for a few weeks. He explained that there was really nothing to do, the schools were closed, most of the families had been evacuated to the countryside where it was hoped that they would be safe if air raids in London started, and the existing residents were enough to cope with the mens and boys clubs. However in the end he agreed to take me on temporarily as a cleaner in the daytime and as an assistant to Hugh Kenyon at the Webbe Boys Club in the evenings. I was to get pocket money of one pound a week. Thus started my time at Oxford House which ended eight years later.

This was July 1940. As there had been no air raid, many families with small children returned to Bethnal Green. The schools remained closed and the children had nothing to do in the streets all day.

Bethnal Green at that time was one of the most densely populated boroughs in London. Almost all the houses were old, mainly in grey brick in terraces of old 'two rooms up and two down' buildings, with a WC in the small backyard. There were often two or more families in a house and space was at a premium. Many people kept hens or rabbits in their backyards, a relic it was sometimes claimed of the Huguenots. There were also one or two rows of weavers' houses in which the communal workshop had occupied the whole of the top floor of several adjoining houses; these certainly derived from the Huguenots. Being foreign refugees they had not been allowed to settle within the walls of the City of London and so moved into Spitalfields and adjoining Bethnal Green.

John Peterson and I were told to do something about the children. We had the daytime use of the Holland Hall but no equipment, and as far as I was concerned no relevant experience. We bought a quantity of sand, several large tin baths and buckets for water, some builder's planks and a few bricks, and we opened the doors in Derbyshire Street. Children poured in and all we could do was to sit on the steps leading down into the hall to keep an eye open for possible accidents or serious quarrels. It was my first experience of 'organising'.

From its earliest days the House had been a pioneer in providing cheap and healthy holidays for the men and boys (aged 14-18) in the clubs by organising camps, usually in the traditional holiday period of the first fortnight of August. In the new war time situation it seemed that the right thing to do was to have an all-age family camp. The problem of the camp site was solved by Guy Clutton-Brock's parents of the use of the extension ground of their house in Oxted in Surrey. The old bell tents and a marquee were set up. 60 local families went down to Oxted by coach. I was given the job of running the canteen. This meant that I went into Oxted at regular intervals to buy stocks of cigarettes, biscuits and sweets, and then opened the canteen to sell twice a day. At night, we were kept awake by the noise of German reconnaissance planes and by search light displays. Weekend evenings were enlivened by the excitement of the teenage girls meeting in the local pubs, the newly arrived Canadian troops, who were stationed nearby. But in general the camp was a success and enjoyed by all.

Soon after the camp was over and we had cleared the site, the Blitzkrieg began the regular nightly air raids on London and particularly on the East End of London with its docks and railway lines. On the first day, it happened to be my day off, I think it was a Saturday, as I started to leave home in north-west London, the sirens went and shortly afterwards the sky to the east took a red glow as it started to reflect the fires. There was no tube connection to Bethnal Green in those days though the tunnel had already been built and I took the normal way back on the No 8 bus. However, it did not go far and I had to make most of the way back by foot through a lurid scene of fires, fire engines and wrecked buildings made all the more dramatic as darkness came on. Bombs were falling, some explosive and others small incendiaries dropped in packets and the noise was increased by the anti-aircraft guns.

Chapter 4
The Air Raid Shelter

In Bethnal Green, some bombs had been dropped and a few fires had started near the House and people were out in the streets asking whether help was needed. This was a feature of all the following nights. Whenever a bomb fell the neighbours immediately came out asking whether and where help was needed. A large number, chiefly old people and mothers with small children, had gathered at the House and asked for shelter there. This posed a difficult dilemma. The official policy was that people should not gather together in large numbers for fear of a lot of casualties if that particular building should be hit. Instead street shelters had been built, unfurnished rectangular buildings of brick and concrete. There was one immediately outside the House in Derbyshire Street, but they were bleak and uncomfortable and little used, except as public lavatories. So our neighbours were allowed in and some sort of sitting, and later, sleeping accommodation was improvised. It first consisted of canvas deck chairs in the Holland Hall. Later there were three tier wooden bunks which filled the small hall and two other rooms in the basement, one of which was reserved for children. The wooden bunks were to be replaced by metal ones. There appeared to be no way in which people could be dissuaded from coming, although the danger was repeatedly pointed out. The reply was that because the House, as distinct from their homes, was large and strong, they wanted to be together, the older ones among them remembered that they had taken shelter there from the Zeppelin raids in the First World War, and above all there had always been good men in the Oxford House and therefore it would not get hit!

In a lengthy article in the *Oxford House Magazine* for October, 1917, there had been a vivid description of how the House became a 'house of defence' during the air raids of 1915, when up to 1,500 people tried to get into the premises and a rule of 'women, children and fathers of families only' had to be enforced.

In the following days and nights news of the 'superior accommodation' at the House spread quickly. The numbers of people seeking to come in each evening grew to such an extent that tickets were issued with those living in the immediate neighbourhood having first choice. Somewhat arbitrarily the limit of people allowed into the shelter was fixed at around 300. We had to man the front door and face the pleading and often angry demands of those who had come from far away. Its popularity was not surprising since those who came quite early in the evening and before the air raid warnings went off, were able to use the canteen. Sing songs and other activities were organised. It was brightly lit and warm, an important matter as the winter came on. The general effect was that the noise made inside blotted out the noise being made by bombs and guns outside. In any case the alternatives were either the bleak street shelters or the arches under the railway most of which had been used as stables for brewery dray horses. These stables were usually still dirty, smelly, cold and unlit and were clearly likely targets for bombs, being under the railway tracks near the main Bethnal Green junction.

As well as providing nightly shelter, the House was designated as a Rest Centre. This meant that when their houses were hit and made uninhabitable, local families came in for some days until more permanent housing could be found for them. The Holland Hall was used for this purpose. Fortunately there were a number of other designated Rest Centres in the Borough. The hall was therefore soon left free for other uses, one of which was the re-registration of children for evacuation to the countryside. Later in the war when there were renewed air raids, the Hall had again had to be used to provide temporary accommodation for homeless families. The nightly presence of some 300 men, women and children meant that someone had to be awake on the alert in case the House itself or a building nearby was hit by a bomb.

One of the small porter's rooms inside the front door was set up as an ARP (Air Raid Precautions) post and one of the resident staff stayed there all night. We took it in two shifts, one from the time the club activities finished around 11 p.m. until 3 a.m. and the other from 3 a.m. to 8 a.m. This meant that each of us had to be on night duty between two and three times a week. The morning shift included waking those sleepers in the shelter who had to go off to work early i.e. from 6 a.m. onwards and also preparing breakfast in the club canteen for those who wanted it. In addition volunteers from the boys club members slept in the second room next to the ARP post. They formed teams of 'fire watchers' in two-hour shifts, two at a time protected only by tin helmets. From the time the sirens sounded until the all clear, they kept watch on the flat roof of the House in case any incendiaries fell nearby. After the first few nights of bombing it had been decided to shut down the Webbe building in Cheshire Street, to concentrate all the club activities in the House and the adjoining mens club premises. Members of the boys club also formed small teams and with a couple of 8mm projectors, which we had begged and borrowed, Mickey Mouse and other similar rented films, went to railway arches and other similar shelters, which had almost no amenities or entertainment, and gave weekly film shows.

For those of us resident at the House, there was much to do in addition to running the normal club activities at night. We often had to improvise in order to respond to new and extraordinary needs. I, for example, was sent off to visit every hardware shop I could find in order to buy chicken wire. Luckily, because of the local tradition of keeping hens in the backyard, there were considerable stocks. We used it to cover all the windows of the lower floors so as to minimise the effect of blast if bombs fell nearby. Another task was to help an elderly couple rescue what furniture they could salvage from the ruins of their house. When we brought it back to store it temporarily in the backyard, I had to go out to buy bottles of paraffin in order to rid it of bugs. The treatment took several days. A less lively, but for me an entirely new experience, was to take a 14 year old from a penniless family to the nearest clothing shop and buy him a whole outfit, suit, shirt, underclothes, socks and shoes so that he could go and apply for his first job. My memory is that it cost fourteen pounds for the lot.

The bedrooms on the top floors of the House were left empty. When the bombing was particularly severe, some of us slept in the kitchen, the only room in the lower floor of the House which was not occupied by shelterers. On occasions I slept on the kitchen table and someone else under it. The story was that I could reach out and get the tin of flea powder which I kept next to me and sprinkle it on myself without waking up. Like most people we slept in our day time clothes and health and hygiene became a problem, more especially when, as a result of particularly heavy bombing the local water supply was cut. We had made the showers and changing rooms in the Holland Hall available to the shelterers. In the emergency, the Fire Brigade came and pumped water into the large tanks in the top of the building.

As the years went on, there was always a possibility that the shelter conditions might give rise to an epidemic of some kind. Guy took advice at the highest level, I think with Lord Horder, the royal physician. As a preventative measure, every one of the shelterers was given an aspirin each evening. It seems to have worked. In general we were looked after by both Dr L'Etang, the very popular local doctor, and by Dr John Lipscombe of the London Hospital, who was John Raven's brother-in-law.

The girls club which Molly Cutton-Brock had successfully revived occupied the two ground floor rooms which had been the common room and the library. After the evening activities were over, those who wished to stayed behind and slept in the bunks which were arranged around the walls. The old dining room and the small hall were for dormitories for men and boys, while two rooms in the basement were for women and children. The Holland Hall in which a boxing ring could be put up was used at different times by the boxing club, for the girls gymnastics and on Saturday nights for dances and entertainments. Every two months or so a 'free and easy' was organised by one of the mens club members, Topper Lee. There was an entrance charge. The programme consisted of songs and other turns by club members and occasional guest performers. Members of the audience were allowed to leave and return again provided they showed their ticket. We were in demand as doormen because the usual reason to leave was to visit the Prince Albert, the pub which stood on the corner of Mape Street and Derbyshire Street, exactly opposite the House. As the evening went on, especially if the singers were not particularly attractive, the visits to the pubs lasted longer and longer. Moreover many of the drinkers were under age, so we had to learn how to deal with a wide range of would-be entrants ranging from the mildly tipsy to the obstreperous and fighting drunk.

It is worth recalling that at this time the normal school-leaving age was fourteen and that a great majority of young Bethnal Greeners started work at that age. Wages in general were low but there were highly paid jobs in salvage work among the ruins of bombed buildings. It was dangerous work and there was an age limit but this was often ignored. For the girls there was unlimited work in the factories making uniforms and other clothing for the armed forces. This meant that quite a few teenagers had more money than they were accustomed to expect. At the same time with most able-bodied men away from their families, the war situation led to an inevitable break in the traditional way of bringing up children. It was in fact in 1939 that the government, recalling the social problems of the 1914-1918 war and facing the prospect of another war, had announced the creation of a National Youth Service. When the war came there was an attempt to introduce compulsory regular attendance at some recognised youth organisation by all those between the ages of 14 and 18. This proved impossible to implement. An attempt was made to make registration of all teenagers compulsory, but this failed too.

In the circumstances it was surprising how smoothly all the various groups using the House managed to pursue their different interests. New rules and sometimes complicated timetables had to be worked out to fit in the use of the hall by the different groups, or the extent to which boys (under 18) could freely use the facilities of the mens club, whose membership consisted mainly of the middle aged and elderly who did not take easily to change in their set leisure time routines.

Chapter 5
The Welsh Schools

When the bombing started, many of the families who had brought their children back from their rural billets during the first half of 1940 wanted their children to leave London again. The Government regulations were that children of school age i.e. 5-14 had to go to the areas designated for their schools, children under 5 had to be accompanied by their mothers and went to other areas. As we started registering them we found a number of families in which there were children both under and above 5 years of age whom their parents did not want to be separated. Some with small children were unwilling to leave their homes and husbands in London. They were not eligible for the official scheme, but we kept a separate register and decided that something should be done to meet their needs.

Most of the rural areas in Southern and Midland England had been designated to receive official evacuees from London and Birmingham. So we had to try further away. John Raven had been on a walking holiday on the Long Myndd and the area west of Shrewsbury. Although it was possible that this area had been reserved for possible official evacuees from Liverpool and Manchester, there had so far been no air raids on those cities, so he took a train to Welshpool. He discovered a large remote but empty house near the village of Llmydiarth in Montgomeryshire. Not only was he able to rent it but also found a competent and willing person to run the House, Mrs. Evan Jones, the widow of a local clergyman.

By October the first all-age group of Bethnal Greeners was installed; with an age range of from 6 weeks to 70! Thus began the history of the Welsh Schools. In time the mainly elderly adults who had been in the first group, returned to London. More children were enrolled. Plas Dolanog, a half-timbered farmhouse a mile or two to the south on the river Vyrwny, was opened as a nursery school for the under fives. Llwydiarth Hall became a school when it was found impossible to send the children to the local chiefly Welsh speaking school. This meant that teachers had to be found, no easy task at that time. Towards the end of the war, a third school for older children was opened at Brampton Bryan in Shropshire, but the educational programme had to be interrupted when the pilotless doodlebug attacks on London triggered another wave of evacuees. Tents were pitched on the lawn and volunteers recruited from university students on vacation. This was typical of the way in which we had to improvise continuously.

John Raven was primarily responsible for the schools, but all of us in different ways and at different times were involved. On one occasion I was at Paddington Station looking for the Shrewsbury train with a small child in my arms, three more clutching my trouser legs and one or two more trailing behind. When the Oxford train came in, out got the history tutor of my Oxford College. "Ah, Peter" he said, "I see that you are getting a far better education than we could give you at Oxford". On another occasion in the winter, Guy, Molly and I arrived at Llanfyllin, the nearest railway station, after the usual wearing journey with changes at Shrewsbury, Oswestry and Gobowen, to find about a foot of snow and no possible transport over the 5 miles to Llwydiarth. So we set off on foot and were thankful to be met by a tractor, the only vehicle that could get through the snow to carry us the last two miles.

As soon as heavy air raids on London became less frequent, parents wanted to have their children back in London. The Welsh schools were an uncomfortable novelty for most of the parents. Boarding schools were unknown in Bethnal Green with the exception of the approved schools to which young delinquents were sent by the sentence of juvenile courts. We tried to meet the reasonable requests of parents to be able to see their children from time to time by arranging for them to make weekend visits. This was no easy matter. Even communication by telephone was difficult; in Llwydiarth there was only one telephone in a public booth. When I rang Llwydiarth in order to make arrangements for a visit, I had to persuade the operator that my call was of national importance, a claim that was sometimes disputed especially when as often happened the operator listened into the ensuing conversation. Transport was even more difficult. Government notices proclaimed; "Is your journey really necessary?". The train connections were often cut or the journeys so delayed that two whole days might be spent just in travelling. Through the generosity of a London business man we had been given a large station wagon car into which could be packed 7 or 8 parents for a weekend visit. The problem then was petrol, which was severely rationed. On one occasion we could obtain only enough to get the car to Wales but nothing for the return journey. At the end of the weekend, the station wagon full of Bethnal Green parents was driven to the nearest Fuel Office in Montgomeryshire. The local official was faced with the choice of issuing petrol coupons or having a car load of Londoners camping in his office. This, however, was a form of blackmail that could only be practised once.

In the later years of the War there was much discussion about the future educational system of the country leading to the new (Butler) Education

Children at play in a street in Bethnal Green

Bethnal Green street scene

21

THE OXFORD HOUSE

Annual Report ~ 1944

Bethnal Green street scene

Act of 1944. Having seen both the benefits and the problems of providing boarding education for London children under the age of 13, John Raven felt that we could also make a contribution to the debate on public schools and democratisation. He contacted the Headmasters of two progressive Public Schools, Dulwich College and Bedales, and got their agreement to take two older boys from the Welsh School and to forego their fees. Finding parents who were willing for their sons to go to these schools proved difficult. In the end only two boys went, one to each school. The boy who went to Bedales came from a typical home, his father was overseas in the army and his mother had to hold down more than a full-time job to support the family. So I found myself having to act as his parent on visiting days and the like. There seemed to be no end to the new experiences I was expected to face.

Chapter 6
Boys Club Work

After Hugh Kenyon left I became 'manager' of the Webbe Boys Club. As such I was also responsible for the boxing section. Like many of the boys clubs, especially those in the East End of London, the Webbe had an immense reputation for boxing. Over the years it had produced champions who had graduated through the London Boys Clubs championships, which were held annually in the Albert Hall, and then to the regional and national levels of the Amateur Boxing Association. I had from time to time to attend the East London regional meetings, which were usually held in a pub at midday on Sunday. At these meetings I was obviously the odd man out, not only because of my age - I was still in my early twenties - , but also because most of the other secretaries were themselves retired boxers and had the marks on their ears and noses to prove it. Less conspicuously I had to go every year to the Albert Hall championships at which one or two Webbe members had usually got through to the finals.

I was also on the committee of the London Federation of Boys Club. Most of the other members were twice as old (or more) as I was. They were representatives of the traditional boys club managers, business or professional men who had been or still were volunteers as part of the philanthropic culture of their 20s and 30s. One of the leading figures was Basil Henriques. After serving in the First World War he and his wife had set up the Oxford and St George's Jewish Settlement and clubs in Stepney. He was the author of a book entitled 'Club Leadership' and was the accepted authority on the subject. On one occasion, when I went into his settlement in Stepney to discuss something, I found myself so overawed by the prospect that I turned back without ever getting to see him.

The general trend in the London and National Boys Club organisations was conservative. As one of the very few young full time club workers it took me some time to have the nerve to make any innovative suggestions. However, as time went on I was able to make some contribution to the Committee's deliberations. In the years immediately after the war, I was chairman of the Leadership Training sub-committee. With the able help of Terence Lawson, formerly club manager of the Aldenham Club in North West London, who joined the London Federation staff as Training Officer, I was able to introduce innovative selection and training methods for both full-time and part-time youth workers. We took as our models the new techniques that had been used by the Army for selecting officers. To see whether these were useful for youth work we got ourselves included in a British Army team on a weekend selection course. It was soon after the end of the war and we found ourselves in a Surrey country house selecting officers for the re-constituted Dutch Army, a process still taking place in England before the Dutch authorities felt able to return to their country.

Many of the boys clubs were linked and financially aided by the Public Schools which, in some cases, had started the clubs as 'missions in the slum'. Thus there was Eton Manor in Hackney, Harrow and the Rugby Clubs in Notting Dale, Tonbridge Club near King's Cross, Crown and Manor Club in Hoxton which was supported by Winchester College, and the Haileybury Club in Stepney. It was at the Haileybury that Clement Attlee, a future Prime Minister, had, as a resident at Toynbee Hall, learned much about the social needs of the East End. The Webbe was linked to Berkhamsted School but the link was tenuous. Every summer a coach load of Webbe boys went to Berkhamsted for a cricket match against the school. This was usually a rather difficult occasion as cricket was not a popular game in the East End of London. The Webbe boys were inevitably defeated even though the School did not field its first team. Both sets of boys found communication difficult. It was usually only after a copious tea and just before departure that any real rapport was achieved.

Football on the other hand was more popular, but the available pitches were either on the eastern or western fringes of London. This entailed long and sometimes complicated train journeys; the London Underground system had then not reached Bethnal Green. I have recollections of spending long, cold and almost always wet Saturday afternoons as the sole supporter on the touchline of the many public football pitches on the bleak and windswept Hackney Marshes. On one or two occasions I had to come to the aid of the referee amid loud threats and indications that some of the players might be hiding knives in their stockings. The Webbe was not very strong at football and was more often than not a loser in the league matches organised by the London Federation. Morale was often low. I remember frequent occasions on which I waited on the platform of Bethnal Green Station for members of the team to turn up. Sometimes they didn't and the team played one or two players short.

Road running at night was a traditional way of keeping fit and also of training for the steeple-chase events organised by the London Fed. As a newly appointed manager, I felt that I should from time to time join the runners. I remember running in the black out with no street lamps down the Bethnal

Green Road into the deserted City to the Bank and back on several winter nights.

To round off the varied series of roles I found myself playing, I recall the frustration of trying to produce a scene from 'Midsummer Night's Dream' with reluctant boys club members in order to take part in the London Federation's annual Shakespeare competition. In the 1930s both the Repton and the Webbe boys had a high reputation for acting. This was mainly due to the enthusiasm and ability of Sir Henry Markham, a senior civil servant at the Admiralty who had been a regular volunteer club helper. Moreover one of the club members, Alfie Bass had gone on to become a professional actor and a star of both stage and screen. This was another instance of my feeling that tradition required me to follow the past example. It was a great mistake. I had no talent as a producer and the cast was unwilling. When we went to perform at the Toynbee Hall theatre it was a disaster.

By 1944 as the regular nightly air raids had become infrequent it became possible to re-open the old Webbe Club building in Cheshire Street. At about the same time Guy Clutton-Brock was persuaded to join the British Military Government administering the sector of Berlin under British control, and be responsible for youth and religious affairs. This led to changes at Oxford House. John Illsley, a former volunteer at the Tonbridge Boys Club, who had succeeded Hugh Kenyon as Vice-Head in 1941, was appointed Acting Head and I took his place as Vice-Head and Secretary to the Council. My place with the boys club was taken by Merfyn Turner, who not only restarted all the club activities in Cheshire Street, but with his own hands reconstructed the top floor into a self-contained flat for his own accommodation. I took over John Illsley's responsibilities for the mens club which was in the middle of a somewhat protracted and painful process of becoming a Community Centre.

The idea of community centres was a new one and had been tentatively floated in a government publication, a little red book. They were primarily seen as useful tools for creating a sense of community in new housing areas. But Guy Clutton-Brock had seen in them a way of formalising his continuing attempts to strengthen the long tradition of self-government by elected committees in the mens and boys clubs. He also saw them as a way to democratise the work of the House, and to throw it open to local Bethnal Greeners with the continuing of activities for all ages and both sexes which had evolved from the pressures of the wartime into the use of the House and Club premises as an air raid shelter for the local community.

Chapter 7
Personalities and Social Work

A very important part of the war time activity was the Unseen Club. This was the creation of Peter Johnson, a pre-war club manger at the Webbe. He came to live at the House while being in charge of personnel management at Sainsbury's as his daytime job. He built up a register of old club members serving in the Forces and maintained a mammoth correspondence with hundreds of them. He had the advantage of knowing many of them personally from his pre-war club work. His bedroom, which was the end one on the first floor, became a museum as well as a carousing clubroom for members on leave. Eventually as it adjoined the mens club canteen a door was made through the intervening wall. This further broke down in a physical way the barriers between residents and Bethnal Greeners.

Another bedroom on the first floor was turned into a common room for residents, all the ground floor being occupied by clubrooms and shelters. It became a routine that when the clubs shut down at 11pm we would all meet there for a hot drink and an exchange of information. John Raven had taken responsibility for our cultural welfare and had produced one of the old-fashioned record players with a big horn. So in addition we had nightly recitals of classical music. After being introduced to the double concerto for violin and cello, I was persuaded that Brahms did not deserve to be called 'gloomy'.

As the war continued, air raid warnings persisted even though the bombing was not as intense locally as it had been in the Blitzkrieg of 1940. The House was eventually officially recognised as an air raid shelter. All the windows on the ground floor were blocked with concrete, and an anti-blast wall was built on the top of the steps leading to the front door from Mape Street. A massive canopy of steel sheeting was put over the whole of the ground floor which was held up by steel pillars going down through the basement. Before this, Guy Clutton-Brock had determined to improve the sleeping accommodation. The wooden bunks were both uncomfortable and unsafe; they were also capable of harbouring bugs. A request through the normal local channels for metal bunks was turned down. Exploiting his status as a former civil servant he went to Whitehall to see Ellen Wilkinson who was the Minister responsible and eventually got her agreement. What he did not tell her was that we had already got the bunks through the goodwill of local metal workshop owners who knew the House and were quite willing to ignore the steel rationing regulations in a good cause.

At Christmas we held a party which was a bit like an old fashioned garden fete with sideshows and competitions in various parts of the buildings. Of these the most popular was the fortune-telling booth which we constructed out of old blankets and curtains in a dark corner of the club billiard-room. John Raven made a convincing fortune teller, tall, dark, swathed in long borrowed drapes and skirt. I acted as ticket collector and kept the queue in order. Since I knew almost all of the customers well I was able to tip him off with some juicy titbit about each of the new enquirers just before they came into his murky presence. He delivered his predictions and warnings in a high screechy voice and, as we were able to smuggle him in and out of his booth, his identity was never discovered. Later on in the evening after closing the side door into the club, he and I manned the front door of the House. By this time many of the club members had spent a lot of their Christmas savings in the Prince Albert and were considerably the worse for wear. The advantage of using the front door was that it was near to the large cloakroom with WCs and washbasins. We soon became adept at wheeling the swaying bodies swiftly there and helping to make them as sober and clean as would justify letting them in to enjoy the rest of the party in the House.

The Oxford House Mutual Loan and Savings Club had been established in 1888 after several of the publicans who were the traditional organisers of Christmas savings clubs had decamped just before pay-out time. Despite a similar departure by one of the earlier secretaries of the Oxford House Club, it had survived and continued throughout the war years and after. Every Saturday afternoon we arranged the Holland Hall so that the honorary club officers could sit at the receipt of custom. At the beginning of the year each member took out and paid for a number of shilling shares. Members were required to pay a weekly subscription. Loans, chiefly to pay for new clothing or bedding, were made without security because everyone was a neighbour or had been at some time. Those who did not take out loans paid a quarterly fine equivalent to the interest they would have paid on a minimum loan. This helped to swell the final amount available for the payout. Some affluent members who had moved away would come about once a month in their large cars to make their deposits. The money was kept in the House safe over the weekend and then taken to the local bank and put into a deposit account to earn interest. Payout was on the second Saturday in December. I recall going up the Bethnal Green Road with Harry Waldron, the Club Secretary, and a policeman especially hired for the occasion, to collect the money from the Midland Bank. In 1945 it amounted to some eighteen thousand pounds which was a considerable amount of money for Bethnal Green in those days. Paying out began at 2 pm and went on until late in the evening. We had to provide tea and biscuits for those involved including the policeman.

Less frequent were the meetings of some friendly societies which used the House for their quarterly or annual meetings. In the days before the creation of the welfare state and the National Health Service, these independent mutual aid organisations played a vital role for many people with low and middle-level incomes. In fact, Beveridge in his original recommendations proposed that they should be retained and used as the basis for the new universal insurance scheme, but this was not accepted. The one that I recall best, because of its historical name was The Society for Refugees from High and Low Normandy. Very few of its members, who presumably were descendants of Huguenot immigrants, lived in Bethnal Green or troubled to come to the meetings. However, according to the rule book which I read with interest, the Secretary was duty bound to visit any member who was housebound because of illness or for any other reason.

Another of the traditional services offered by the House from its earliest days was the Poor Man's Lawyer. Every Friday evening a small volunteer team of lawyers gave free legal advice. This was the forerunner of the official legal aid system though at the time there was no financial or other support for taking a case to court. I recall Brian Jacquet as being the most devoted of the lawyers turning up on his bicycle even in the worst of air raids and having sometimes to stay the night since it was too dangerous for him to attempt to return home in West London.

Chapter 8
Station Disaster

One of the people who walked the streets even in the heaviest of air raids was Sir Wyndham Deedes in his capacity of Chief Air Raid Warden for Bethnal Green. As a former resident and Vice-Head and currently a member of the Council he knew the House well. We were an official ARP post and one of us was on duty every night. On one occasion when it was my turn he turned up around 2am. There did not appear to be any bombing aimed at Bethnal Green though there was plenty of anti-aircraft fire. He suggested that we should go for a walk; he was apparently quite fearless. Compton Mackenzie somewhere recounts how in the First World War Captain Deedes, as he then was, would terrify his fellow officers at Gallipoli by strolling up and down the beach and holding them in deep conversation under heavy shell fire. In my case it was not shellfire so much as bits of shrapnel from anti-aircraft fire which clattered down on the empty streets as we walked under the railway and through Stepney. He wanted to tell me about the 17th century German mystic authors whose works he had been reading when he could not sleep and was not on duty. I had difficulty in even pretending to listen since, though we were both equipped with regulation tin helmets, he never wore his and out of deference I felt I could not put mine on.

Anti-aircraft fire was to play a big part in one of the worst war time tragedies in Bethnal Green. The Underground railway tunnel from Liverpool Street (now the Central Line) had been built but there were no rails. Like many Tube Stations in Central London Bethnal Green Station, still unfinished, was opened as an air raid shelter. In the early evenings, when the weather was fine and there were no raids, having prepared their sleeping space on the platforms, people would come up to the surface to enjoy the fresh air. On one such evening the sirens suddenly started up and almost at the same time the battery of anti-aircraft guns stationed nearby started to fire. The noise of the guns was often more frightening than the noise of bombs exploding. There was a sudden rush to get down into the shelter. The stairway from the street was still in a rough state. A woman with a child stumbled and fell and the crowd behind piled up on top of her. In the ensuing chaos several hundred people were killed and wounded. Immediately afterwards rumours started circulating about a deliberate plot by unknown agents. In any case there was a natural desire to discover how the accident had happened and who was responsible.

The authorities announced that an enquiry would be held behind closed doors. At this point Guy Clutton-Brock intervened and persuaded them that it should be held in public. Since several of the club members had lost relatives, I spent much of the next two weeks attending funeral services in various cemeteries around East London.

Guy's successful intervention was also evidence of success in improving relations between the House and the Borough Council. The Council was 100% Labour, although the local MP was still Sir Percy Harris, a relic from the Liberal past. The Leader of Council, Councillor Tate was traditionally suspicious of what he saw as the interference of do-gooders from the upper classes. In addition, during the pre-war period Michael Seymour, while Head of Oxford House, had served as an independent Borough Councillor in opposition to the Labour majority. However, when it became clear that, with backing from Oxford House, John Peterson genuinely wished to make University House an independently locally governed Settlement, Tate agreed to become Chairman. It was also clear that there were profound changes at Oxford House itself, and, as Mayor, Councillor Tate and his wife, also a Councillor, were persuaded to come and see for themselves.

Historically Oxford House had been established to be essentially an Anglican Christian institution. This was most apparent from the composition of its Governing Council and by the existence of the chapel at the top of the building, clearly designed to represent an Oxford College Chapel. In the 20th Century efforts to appoint a clergyman as head of the House failed or were very short-lived. In asking Guy Clutton-Brock to act as Head, I do not know whether the Council was aware that he had at one time thought of being ordained but then drew back. During the War some residents were Anglicans and others like myself were not. It did not seem to matter.

A recurrent issue was what to do about club activities on Sunday evenings. Sunday dances in the Holland Hall were very popular. For a while an attempt was made to make entry to the dance conditional on having attended a short service in the chapel beforehand. It was very short, usually not more than 10-15 minutes long. We took it in turns to read something whether biblical or not. However it was a flop. First of all there had to be some method of determining who had been there. Tickets could be exchanged so we tried marking wrists with rubber date stamps, but that seemed ridiculous. In any case there was no point if most of those attending did so reluctantly and continued to chatter and giggle throughout. So the whole thing was dropped. As far as the residents themselves were concerned there was a time for communal silent prayer and meditation in the chapel everyday after breakfast for those who wanted to come; some did, others did not.

Guy Clutton-Brock himself was an active member of a small local fellowship made up of those in charge of local Settlements which met regularly. One outcome of this was that for a number of weeks he and Charles Howarth, who was at the Quaker Centre in Barnet Grove, took 'soapboxes' out into the Sunday market in Brick Lane and tried to preach to the huge crowds there. It was not a success. Guy's commitment was obvious in Bethnal Green and afterwards when he went on to work first in post-war Germany and later in Africa. He summed up his personal belief most movingly in the last Annual Report he wrote at Oxford House for the year 1943-4. He wrote of 'being compelled by the spirit of Christ' and ended up by quoting Canon Barnett – 'our settlement will rest on a secure foundation only so far as it is based on Love – Love strong enough to stand the strain of working with little or no apparent result, broad enough to sink differences in one common purpose'.

Chapter 9
The Post War Years

During the war years and immediately afterwards there were changes among the staff and residents, as well as a number of significant visitors. Brian King came for several years during the war. He was a law don at Pembroke College, Cambridge, seconded for war service to work in the Home Office in the department responsible for approved schools. I think that he found the informal atmosphere of the club canteen an enjoyable and useful adjunct to his new duties. His tall and always calm figure made him popular with club members. Gordon McCarthy came to stay when on leave from the RAF. Later he was demobilised and started training as an accountant. When there was an interregnum in the postwar years he was acting Head of the House before leaving for a distinguished career in tea estate management in Assam. Another postwar resident was Peter Duke, who became an outstanding manager of the Webbe, and after being Head of the House went on to be the first Principal of the National Youth Leadership Training Centre at Leicester.

For a short period early in the war Penelope Jessel came to be housekeeper and cook and then left to join the ATS, the women's branch of the Army. Later she became a leading figure in the Liberal Party and a DBE. Among the regular volunteer helpers in the girls club was Margaret Higginson, a teacher at St. Paul's High School for Girls. She later went on to become Head of Bolton High School. She found the Bethnal Green teenage working girls an instructive contrast to her more middle-class pupils. One evening she bought one of them, Shirley Catlin. After they had spent an evening with the girls club, I recall talking to the future Baroness Williams about the work of the House over a mug of cocoa in the kitchen.

When Molly Clutton-Brock gave up work with the girls club to have a baby, she had a number of successors, one of whom, Betty Foxell married one of the first post-war foreign visitors to the House. He was Phokion Plytas, a Greek who was given a British Council scholarship as a reward for his work with the British parachutists dropped in occupied Greece. Subsequently after working with the BBC Overseas Service, he became a successful television actor, most often portraying a gangster or villain. Another

European visitor was Otto Krabbe, the Head of the University Settlement in Copenhagen. He became a personal friend of several of us and made repeated visits, I stayed with him both at the Copenhagen Settlement and in the 1960s when he became principal of a training centre for Danish social workers.

The House also became a place where students of social administration at the London School of Economics came to get practical experience. Among the first of these were two African students, perhaps the first African residents in the history of the House. One of them James Riby-Williams eventually joined the United Nations staff and became Regional Youth Officer for Africa, and thus a colleague of mine when I too joined the UN and visited him in 1966 in Addis Ababa.

In the autumn of 1945, the time had come for me to return to Oxford. In 1939 and 1940 I had only completed half of the Greats degree course, and my college had kept my scholarship open for me to return. However I no longer wanted to study Classics and Philosophy and at that time the University had not yet recognised Sociology or similar subjects. Moreover as there was so much to do in Bethnal Green I decided to stay on. Later the University granted me a degree on the basis of my earlier academic work and my 'war service'.

As an effort to revive the links between Bethnal Green and Oxford, John Peterson and I devised a 3 week training course which we called 'Discover Your Neighbour' to be held at the end of the University year. The assumption was that while graduates knew all about their various professional studies in medicine, law, administration and so on, they had little or no real understanding of their future clients. We recruited a group of some 7-8 who had just passed their final exams. We sent them out individually on various assignments – to spend a day with a rent collector, to work in a local bakery or as a cleaner in the Bethnal Green Hospital or on the beat with a policeman. We exploited our local contacts. At the end of each day, the whole group met together to exchange experiences and to discuss the implications under the leadership of a tutor who was trained in anthropology. One of the fascinating outcomes was to see how differently those trained for different professions experienced the same assignment when their turn came. Thus, for example, the law student and the medical student brought back quite different impressions from their respective days in the hospital. 'Discover Your Neighbour' ran successfully for three years and then faded out because of lack of applicants.

Before the advent of the welfare state one of the organisations which provided a vital service for families without normal means of economic support was the Charity Organisation Society, the COS. This had been formed in the mid-19th Century to organise philanthropy and to deal with the relief of poverty in a scientific manner. In some local circles COS had come to stand for 'Cringe or Starve'! I became a member of the local committee which met in a small office in Hoxton Square amid the furniture makers and upholstery workshops. We would adjudicate on cases which were presented by a small team of trained social workers. Again this was a committee on which I found myself the odd man out, both because the other members were all ladies and because they were at least twice my age. Although COS did not have large funds of its own, it had access to a range of both local and national charities and organisations which had money earmarked for different kinds of need and its recommendations were usually accepted. The committee tended to be severe in its determination of need. I recall a discussion as to whether one shilling a week to cover the rental of a wired wireless, which was to be found in most homes in those days, was a permissible item of expenditure in calculating a families budget. I should add that the COS itself was certainly not an ungenerous organisation.

Through its Director Ben Astbury, who was responsible for the allocation of much of the financial aid which was sent from the US for British welfare organisations, the Welsh Schools were adopted by the Woolworth Company of America and all their costs covered. In addition through his help, large crates would arrive from the USA. I recall one full of jars of homemade jam and another with dozens of beautiful hand-knitted patchwork blankets, donated by housewives from all over America and sent through the Aid to Britain Fund. In later years the COS changed its name to FWA, the Family Welfare Association.

Chapter 10
Youth and Community Work

It had not been the custom for any of the clubs to be open on a Sunday during daytime. However because of the extraordinary conditions created by the attempted resurgence of the fascist movement under Sir Oswald Mosley, the Webbe Building was opened around midday on Sundays. The boys were encouraged to come in rather than stay outside in the streets. The corner of Cheshire Street, with its proximity to Whitechapel which still had a predominant Jewish population, was the favourite battlefield for the fascists who would try to hold a meeting there, and the militant left wing and Jewish groups which were opposed to them. Large numbers of police were brought in in an attempt to keep the peace and hold the two sides apart. The windows of the first and second floor of the Webbe building provided a grandstand view of the mêlée and the often not so neutral stance of the police. In the 1930s, the Lotingas, Jewish twin brothers, had started the Cambridge and Bethnal Green Boys Club, which had a rule that its membership should be half Jewish and half non-Jewish as an attempt to combat the rise of local fascism. This had survived the War under non-Jewish leadership. In general over the years I did not encounter anti-Semitism as any kind of problem. Though sometimes a topic of discussion, the fact that I and the others at the House were pacifists was never an obstacle.

One of the effects of opening the House to whole families during the air raids was to underline the need to make provision for all ages. Otherwise unused during the daytime, the Holland Hall was turned into a day nursery. Among its members was Sally Clutton-Brock who had been born in 1943 and was probably the first child christened in the Oxford House Chapel. As a very small baby she was put in her carrycot on a shelf which was built out from one of the windows of the Clutton-Brooks' flat high up on the third floor of the House overlooking Mape and Derbyshire Street. When the weather turned threatening, the neighbours would come out onto the street and call up to Molly to take the baby in before the rain came. The day nursery flourished. It was later transferred to the University House premises in Victoria Park Square.

The tradition of the boy clubs was that the age limit of 14 to 18 should be strictly observed. This meant that there were always many small boys under age clamouring to be let in. We decided that a possible solution was to start a separate junior club and this had been a success, run by Roy Stevens, a young pacifist and Cambridge graduate who joined the staff. After the war we launched a movement to spread the creation of junior i.e. children's' clubs in out of school hours. The time seemed propitious. Lady Allen of Hurtwood had brought back from Denmark the idea of Junk playgrounds, afterwards dignified with the title of Adventure Playgrounds. The Save the Children Fund agreed to support a supervised playground next to the University House. On a national scale we formed the National Under Fourteens Association with W. W. Astor MP as Chairman. For a while we were able to employ a full time organising secretary, the Astors having lent their house in Carlton House Terrace for a fundraising piano concert given by Harriet Cohen.

For the 14 – 18 age groups, as part of the National Youth Service, the London County Council had established a network of Borough Youth Committees. In Bethnal Green it did not function very well. Most of us attended its meetings only because the LCC as the local education authority was the source of annual grants for youth work. Typically for the times there were no young people on the Youth Committee. Officially recognised youth organisations did not include any of the political movements. With the enthusiasm engendered by the wartime alliance with the Soviet Union, added to the traditional socialism of the East End, the Young Communist League's local branch was one of the most lively youth groups, but was excluded. In their disappointment some of them came to us for advice and we tried to maintain this contact. At the official level, young people's representation was channeled into Youth Councils, but when the young members tried to attend the meetings of the Youth Committee itself, they were of course refused. We found ourselves acting as advisors to activists and thus provoked much reproof and headshaking from the long-suffering LCC official Youth Officers for the district. I recall at some point holding the fort in a small vacant shop in the Bethnal Green Road which the dissident Youth Council had taken as its headquarters.

Another less controversial but in the end equally abortive campaign was one to turn unused bombed sites into small vegetable gardens. Initial enthusiasm among the children and young people soon waned. The soil, when it could be excavated from the ruins, proved infertile. Any seedlings that broke through were quickly vandalised or destroyed by the traffic fumes and the contributions of stray cats and dogs.

Club members returning from the Forces often found it hard to find jobs. Some decided to become London taxi drivers. Then as now a taxi driver's licence was only given after he had passed a very stiff examination of 'The Knowledge'. I spent several hours armed with a London A-Z atlas helping would-be cabbies to memorise street names and the quickest route from one place in town to another. Happily several succeeded and for years afterwards I had from time to time the delightful experience of being hailed by a cabbie rather than having to hail a cab.

After leaving the RAF one of the old Webbe boys started a coffee stall which he set up nightly in the Bethnal Green Road. Merfyn Turner and I noticed that, when we went there late at night for a hot drink, there was usually a small crowd around it made up of boys who had been excluded from the Webbe for their inability to keep to the rules or for being members of a gang. They did not resent our presence. In fact we were able to get on well with most of them. This led to our growing interest in the so called 'unclubables'. Helped by John Spencer, a Probation Officer, who on leaving the army had come to reside at the House, and with the support of some of his colleagues in the Probation Service, and of Professor Herman Mannheim at the LSE, we undertook some research. This led us to the conclusion that many of the unclubables were in fact trying to join something but could not find the right kind of club. This also tied in with the formation of small often delinquent gangs.

With the financial backing of the London Parochial Charity, and entirely dependent on Merfyn Turner's deep concern and brilliant ability to work with delinquents of all kinds, we started the Barge Boys Club on a Thames sailing barge moored off a bombed site at Wapping. This was a pioneer experimental project which lasted for 5 years and attracted a great deal of attention. To the astonishment of the gang who used the club, Queen Mary, the Queen Mother, agreed to pay for the purchase of a boat so that they could compete in Thames side regattas. In a probably unique correspondence conducted through one of her ladies-in-waiting, the boys wrote to thank for the gift and asked whether they could name the boat, 'Queen Mary'. This was turned down and the Queen's suggestion of 'Endeavour' was adopted. In 1948, Merfyn moved from the Webbe to live on the Barge and a few years later, he started up Norman House as one of the first houses for homeless discharged prisoners. There was a strong Oxford House connection since both John Illsley and I served on the Norman House Committee for some years.

The usefulness of a coffee stall as a focal point to attract young people and to undertake 'unattached' youth work remained in my mind. Merfyn and I had in fact bought a coffee stall, but we were never able to get the necessary permission from the police and the local authorities to operate where we wanted to. So we sold it. I kept the idea on ice until some time later, when

I was undertaking a training course for the London YWCA, they decided to take it on. Through their influential connections with the women police they were able to get permission to set up the coffee stall in Paddington. The coffee stall project ran from 1960 to 1965 and attracted support from the Department of Education and Science as well as several major trusts. It was written up in a book entitled 'Working with Unattached Youth' (Routledge and Kegan Paul 1967) by George Goetschius and Joan Tash. It became an important signpost at both theoretical and practical levels in the development of youth work.

Another similar publication 'Working with Community Groups' (1969) was derived from work on the new postwar housing estates around London in which I had become involved in the post War period. This activity took place at two levels both inspired and led by Muriel Smith of the London Council of Social Services. I was interested both because of the problems we were facing establishing a community centre set-up at Oxford House, and also because many Bethnal Green families were moving out to new estates. Some of these estates were provided with community halls. Since most of the residents of the estate were newcomers there was no communal experience which might guide the running of these centres, unlike Bethnal Green where many families had been neighbours for several generations. In order to provide training in committee work we adopted the new technique of sociodrama and ran a kind of traveling circus in which we held mock committee meetings taking on different, often stereotyped, roles followed by audience participation and discussion.

At a more administrative level we formed a small group made up of town planners and social workers. Many of the derelict areas of inner London were about to be rebuilt and a large number of housing estates were at the planning stage. There were issues of high or low density reconstruction and of the extent to which Londoners' would take to or benefit from living in high-rise buildings, as well as questions as to whether in the tidying up process, awkward but popular institutions like street markets should be forbidden. We called the group the Kenilworth Club because we met in the comfort of the hotel of that name. The group had no formal existence and sometimes had illegal access to plans before they were in the public domain. I think it had some impact in getting plans modified on the basis of the frontline experience of the social workers. That the Kenilworth Club was not altogether effective in some of the larger issues can be seen with hindsight from the failure of tower blocks and the chronic social problems of some of the housing estates.

The changes at the House continued. Sir Walter Moberly resigned as Chairman of the Council and was succeeded by the Dean of Westminster,

Alan Don. As Secretary to the Council I had the pleasure of meetings in the Jerusalem Chamber at Westminster Abbey. However in contrast to that medieval environment, pressure from the Committee of the Community Centre to be represented on the Council was mounting. It seemed to me to be a logical and welcome development. In due course Charles Wastell, who had been a Webbe Club boy when I arrived in 1940 and had now returned from serving in the RAF, became the first Bethnal Green member. Meanwhile there had been another unsuccessful attempt to find a suitable clerical Head of the House. I was nearing the point of what would now be called 'burn out' and decided I should move on.

Chapter 11
Moving On

The BBC advertised for someone to take charge of programmes for Youth. At the time the only programmes billed as youth programmes were scripted discussion groups with professional adult actors reading their parts as young participants. I applied. The interview was less than complimentary but I was invited to spend a day with the producers of the Schools programmes, after which I went to a second interview. The BBC then announced that no appointment would be made.

Two weeks later, one of the producers telephoned to ask whether I was serious in claiming that an unscripted discussion group made up of real young people on topics of interest to them could make a good programme. I said I was and we arranged that I should contact some ten young people whom I did not previously know. I did this with the help of the local club leaders in the East End. One evening, we all went up to a recording studio in the basement of a building in Piccadilly, which had been a night club before the war. The sound engineers set up their apparatus and we started, but there was a curious background noise in what was supposed to be a soundproof studio. After some minutes there was a loud bang and all the electric power failed, the noise stopped as did all attempts at recording. The young people had an enjoyable and noisy time in the total darkness while finding their way out. It emerged that in a neighbouring basement, a workman with a pneumatic drill had been breaking up bombproof walls which had been put in and had put the drill through the main power cable. Luckily he was not seriously shocked. I gave the young participants their fares home, thanked them for their help and left them to the excitement of exploring Piccadilly Circus. The BBC men invited me for a drink in a nearby bar.

This was not quite the end of my broadcasting career. Some months later, prompted by one of the BBC people, the Head of Broadcasting at UNESCO, contacted me and invited me to chair a series of unscripted discussions with a group of overseas students from Asian, African and Latin American countries who were in the UK. With the help of the British Council I found volunteers. The six sessions focused on how the different cultural viewpoints affected relationships between the students and their hosts. They were recorded and broadcast from a number of radio stations around the world.

About this time in the summer of 1948 I applied for and to my astonishment got a Research Fellowship in Youth Policies and Programmes at Bristol University. My astonishment was due to the fact that at the house party style of selection which was the new fashion at the time, several of my fellow applicants were academically qualified while I was not. The post was the first of its kind and for the next seven years I was able both at Bristol and abroad to make effective use of the practical experience I had gained in Bethnal Green.

So I left the Oxford House after eight years which had totally re-oriented my life. Had I continued with my Oxford studies in Litterae Humaniores, I would probably have ended up as a dull civil servant or perhaps as an unhappy academic. Instead I had been given unparalleled field training in Youth and Community work which over the next 50 years took me to more than 100 different countries around the globe in an ever-changing career which I always enjoyed. Most importantly I had learnt unforgettable lessons from my contacts with people like Guy Clutton-Brock and from the hundreds of men, women and children whom I got to know at Oxford House.